Flash – A Memoir

Written by
Roy Sennett

Edited by
Emma Engers

Illustrated by
Nicci Martin

Grosvenor House
Publishing Limited

The right of Roy Sennett to be identified as the author of this
work has been asserted in accordance with Section 78
of the Copyright, Designs and Patents Act 1988

The book cover is copyright to Roy Sennett

This book is published by
Grosvenor House Publishing Ltd
Link House
140 The Broadway, Tolworth, Surrey, KT6 7HT.
www.grosvenorhousepublishing.co.uk

A CIP record for this book
is available from the British Library

ISBN 978-1-83975-989-5

This book is dedicated to all dog lovers,
and particularly to our family who were privileged
to have grown up with this unique dog.

He provided us with many hours of entertainment,
joy, and trouble, but was a true legend of his time.
This book was written to preserve the memories
of our much loved Rat Terrier, Flash.

Intro

Many people see a dog as *just a pet*, something easily replaceable. If you are one of those people, this story might confuse you. You might be wondering how you could possibly write an entire book about a pet dog.

If, like me, you understand how a dog can become a part of the family, an extra child and a friend, then this book should make sense to you, and I hope that you enjoy it. And to those of you feeling confused, I hope that by the end of this book you will understand what I mean, and perhaps see things a bit differently. Because this is the story of a dog who was never just a pet, and definitely wasn't replaceable. Even today, almost twenty years after he left us, his memory lives on through the people who knew him. I should probably mention that these aren't all good memories – some are, without a doubt, the sort of memories you would try to repress – but it cannot be denied that Flash made an impact on every single person who crossed paths with him.

A troublemaker, an escape artist, a fearless explorer with a predisposition for dangerous situations.

But also a loyal and protective friend, who loved his family more than anything.

Flash was no ordinary dog.

And after reading this memoir, I'm sure you will agree.

Chapter 1
The story begins

Our story begins way back in 1977. My wife, Barbara, and I had just arrived in England. We were both born and raised in South Africa, but after getting married, we decided to make the move to London. I had worked there as a dentist a few years earlier, so I was fairly familiar with the city, and we were both excited to settle down and start a family there.

This is still a while before Flash enters the scene, but I first want to give you some context and background for the story. Also, I'm a big believer in the power of coincidence, and you'll notice that I mention a number of coincidences throughout this book. Here is the first.

I was looking to buy a dental practice in London. I still clearly remember Betty Philpot – she had a dental recruitment and sales agency, and knew everything and everyone connected with the dental profession in London. I told her that ideally I was looking for a practice in the West End, and she found me a great spot in Harley Street, where a prominent dentist, Dr Smith, was selling his practice at a very reasonable price. But there was a catch – he would only sell to someone that he felt was "right" for his practice.

Hoping that I might be that "right" person, I applied and went in for an interview. I remember wearing my blazer and striped tie, with well-shined shoes (of course). But right from the start of the interview I could tell that my chances were slim – Dr Smith spoke the Queen's English, while there I was with my broad South African accent. After half an hour I was very relieved to leave.

But the next day I got a phone call from Betty, telling me that I had been short-listed, and that I should come in for a second interview. This was quite a surprise, but I figured that I had nothing to lose, so I went to this second interview feeling much calmer and more relaxed. And I actually seemed to get on much better with Dr Smith this time.

Then, out of the blue, he asked me if I had any relatives in the UK. I replied that I did not, and he looked somewhat puzzled, saying he was sure he recognised my surname. As if this wasn't confusing enough, he then asked me if my father was a dentist, and mentioned his first name!

My father was a dentist, and it transpired that he and Dr Smith had shared a tent in North Africa during World War II! What are the odds, you might be asking yourself. I can tell you that they are incredibly small, which is why I wanted to include this coincidence in the story. Unsurprisingly, Dr Smith decided that I should be the person to have his practice.

At the time, however, the dentist I was working for advised me to rather buy a family practice in the suburbs, and I followed his recommendation, which turned out to be a very good move.

The property in question was a detached double-fronted house in Ealing, with a surgery downstairs and a flat upstairs. This setup was very convenient, but also had its disadvantages. Especially when patients knew that I lived above the surgery and would come by with emergencies at all hours. Also, this is proof that working from home is definitely not a new concept.

Chapter 2
Enter Flash

After a few difficult years, and a lot of hard work, we were able to buy a house near the surgery. Now that we were more settled, Barbara suggested that this might be a good time to get a dog. Yes, I thought, what an excellent idea! We had both grown up with dogs, and both agreed that it would be a great addition to our family. However, it seems this is where our agreement ended, as we had very different ideas about what sort of dog we should get.

When picturing our future pet, the qualities I had in mind were pretty standard, or so I thought. Obedient, playful, healthy, loyal, a dog that you could really bond with. I imagined us playing in the park, and spending time together at home. I wanted a dog that I could proudly take for walks around the neighbourhood. Nothing too controversial, I'm sure you'll agree.

Barbara, on the other hand, always had a soft spot for abandoned dogs. She liked the idea of finding one that had had a really tough life, and giving it a second chance. So she had her heart set on getting a dog from an animal welfare organisation.

I'll give you a moment to guess who got their way in the end.

I still clearly remember the day I arrived home from the surgery to find a medium-size, not particularly handsome, black, mixed breed dog, limping around our house. The cherry on top was finding out that his name was Flash. Flash the limping dog! Barbara explained that the limp was due to the fact that he had been thrown from a car. This traumatic experience also meant that he was very nervous of people. Amazing, I thought, just the type of dog I had in mind…

8 months old, 80% Jack Russel, 20% unknown (or so we thought at the time) – a mongrel through and through. Definitely not the dog I had in mind, but it turns out he was just the dog we all needed. I didn't know it at the time, but this would be the start of over two decades of exciting, terrifying, hilarious, drama-filled, unforgettable, and truly incredible years.

Let's start by focusing on the drama-filled part. In fact, just two days after we adopted Flash, the drama began. I was at home, sitting in the lounge, when I suddenly heard the screeching of brakes, followed by a loud crash. I rushed to the front door to see what had happened, and discovered that two cars had smashed into each other right outside my house. Luckily neither driver was injured, but I went out to see if I could be of any assistance. One of the drivers angrily told me that a small black dog had run across the road, and he'd had to brake at the last minute to avoid hitting him. Unfortunately the car behind him had not braked quickly enough.

By this time the mysterious black dog was far off in the distance, and the driver demanded to know who it belonged to.

Well, I was reasonably confident that it wasn't Flash, as the dog in question quickly disappeared down the street, no limp in sight. It was, of course, later that day that I discovered that Flash's limp had miraculously healed…

And it turned out that the name Flash was actually rather appropriate – without the limp he was a very fast dog. Possibly even fast enough to run across the road, narrowly avoiding being hit, and then escape down the street before he could be identified. Luckily the drivers were insured and never took the matter further, so Flash got away with it. This time.

Conveniently for a dog owner, we lived opposite a park, and Flash absolutely loved running around there. Even more so, he loved annoying the other dogs there. His favourite game was to get underneath the large dogs, bite their legs, and then run away before they could stop him. As well as being fast, he could also change direction very quickly, so he was extremely unpopular, and almost impossible to catch.

However, his love for running also got him into some scary situations. I still remember the time we took him to Horsenden Hill, and he misjudged the end of the cliff. He was going so fast that he couldn't stop in time, and went hurtling right over the edge. My heart was racing in my chest as I watched him literally flying through the air, but as soon as his feet touched down on the ground he just continued running, as if nothing had happened. I think I was more shaken than he was.

The more time I spent with Flash, the more his personality began to show. I discovered that he was a very curious (some might say nosy) dog, and he enjoyed exploring the neighbourhood (unkinder people might have called it breaking and entering). Especially the breaking part. The most expensive item he managed to break (that I know of) was a neighbour's priceless vase. In his defence, the incident was clearly an accident – Flash only knocked the vase over because he was running away in a panic, having been frightened by the neighbour (who had just come across a strange dog in his house). Unfortunately the neighbour didn't see it this way, and I ended up having to replace the vase at my own expense.

While he enjoyed raiding the neighbours' houses, Flash did a pretty good job of guarding our own house. He would always bark whenever someone rang the doorbell. He was still very nervous though, and the thought of strangers entering the house must have put him further on edge, because as well as barking, he would let out the most awful fart. Not only was it potent and pungent, but it seemed to linger in the air for hours. And then, to make matters worse, he had a habit of disappearing just as I opened the door, leaving me engulfed in noxious fumes. This led to numerous awkward and embarrassing explanations. And it was usually pretty clear that the person at the door did not buy the "It was my invisible dog" excuse.

Flash also succeeded in throwing me off guard a number of times. One of these times was when I had put an advert in the Dental Journal for a dental nurse, and was interviewing candidates. This was also soon after our son, Richard, had been born, and it was mandatory for the local maternity nurse to visit.

It started with the doorbell ringing, and Flash performing his usual hat-trick of barking, farting, and disappearing. I opened the door to see a woman whose face very quickly distorted as the fumes wafted towards her. She said she was a nurse so I quickly ushered her in, trying to hide my embarrassment, and apologising for the smell caused by my very nervous dog, which she clearly wasn't buying.

Things got progressively worse when I started asking her about her experience with dental patient care, and various dental products and procedures. She told me that she had no dental experience, and I was about to ask why she had bothered coming for this interview, when she said that she was here to see our newborn son, Richard. This time it was impossible to hide my embarrassment, so with a very red face, I sent her upstairs to Barbara.

Chapter 3
The move

After a few years we decided to move out of Ealing. We found a house in Pinner in a cul-de-sac in a peaceful neighbourhood, which looked ideal. Pinner also seemed like a good choice, as we had many friends in the surrounding areas. The house was detached, with a large back garden, which backed onto the river Pin. We didn't know this at the time, but the river would flood every couple of years, and when it burst its banks the water overflowed into our garden, turning it into a swamp.

By this time Flash was truly one of the children in our family – the naughtiest child by far. So I made sure that the perimeter of the garden was fenced off. This made it quite secure, or so I thought.

I remember our first day in Pinner after the move.

There was a knock on my door, and I was pleasantly surprised to see a man who told me that he lived a few houses away and would like to introduce himself. What a friendly neighbourhood, I thought to myself. But then, the words I dreaded hearing – he asked me if I had a dog. I could see from his facial expression that this wasn't going to end well. He proceeded to tell me that a dog had attacked his cat earlier that day. I said that I was very sorry to hear this, but assured him that it couldn't possibly be our dog. Flash had now appeared from the lounge, wagging his tail and looking quite innocent. The man went on to explain that he had seen a small black dog with his cat in its mouth, and that the cat had only narrowly escaped the incident, with a large patch of its fur missing.

I promised to keep a watchful eye on Flash, and asked the man to let me know if there were any more issues. I also searched the house for cat fur after he left, but luckily there was no evidence to be found.

It was winter when we moved, and I remember the rain pelting down in the freezing cold, as we tackled the tasks of unpacking boxes and sorting out furniture and clothes. It was very likely this combination of freezing temperatures and continual downpour, along with the stress of the move, that caused me to get a rather nasty cold. Coming home from work one evening, all I could think about was climbing into a nice warm bed. But just as I got comfortable, Barbara said that she could hear Flash barking loudly outside. I told her to let him into the house, as it was pouring.

But he didn't come inside, and his barks suddenly turned to yelps, so I realised something must be wrong. I got dressed, grabbed my torch, and ventured into the back garden to look for him. Flash loved exploring the terrain, so he could be practically anywhere.

After searching frantically, I finally found him, but to my horror, discovered that he was entangled in the wire mesh in the river, with the water level rising fast. I shouted to Barbara to bring my toolbox, where I had a pair of wire cutters. I have no idea how long it took, but I somehow managed to get him free, without either of us falling into the river Pin and being swept away. I'm also amazed that I didn't contract pneumonia from that ordeal.

The next day I did some repair work to better secure the back garden.

But unknown to me, Flash had managed to burrow under the wire perimeter fence, so that he could escape and wander off to explore the neighbourhood. He was often seen walking down Pinner High Street, and people were astonished to see him cross at the pedestrian crossing. He even became well-known by shopkeepers, who would give him treats when he walked past. Again, we had no idea this was happening, but Flash had become quite the celebrity of Pinner High Street.

In fact, when my mother-in-law came to visit from South Africa, she felt like she was famous when taking Flash for a walk down the High Street, amazed that so many shopkeepers knew him and were so happy to see him.

A few years after our move to Pinner, there was an especially bad winter downpour, and many of the back gardens in our street were flooded, our own back garden included.

Besides the obvious difficulty of having part of your property turned into a marshland, a bigger problem that our neighbours seemed to be facing was an infestation of rats that had run up from the burst river bank. As you can imagine, this caused much panic among the houses in our cul-de-sac, so we all met to discuss the matter and decided to call in pest control to deal with the problem for the whole street.

I remember watching the pest control inspector moving from house to house, assessing the extent of the infestation. When he reached our house, he was surprised that our rat problem was nowhere near as bad as our neighbours'. We spoke for a few minutes about the possible reasons for this, when Flash walked into the room, and the inspector suddenly smiled. He said the reason we weren't infested was obvious – we had a Rat Terrier, and he pointed at Flash.

He explained that these types of dogs were bred to hunt small animals, such as rats and squirrels, and although he couldn't be certain, he said that he was pretty sure that Flash was a Rat Terrier.

We were all very grateful to Flash for keeping our house free from rats, and he definitely received more treats than usual that winter. I never followed up on the suggestion that he might be a Rat Terrier though – we still just considered him our mixed breed mystery.

It was only many years later, when I was looking at some old photographs, specifically one of Flash staring up a tree at a squirrel, that I remembered the name Rat Terrier, and decided to do a bit of research.

A quick Google search showed me countless photos of dogs that looked just like Flash. And a few more minutes of searching confirmed that Flash was definitely a Rat Terrier. From his build, to his behaviour, to his temperament – it all matched perfectly.

In fact, the more I read, the more it all made sense. His intelligence and curiosity, his agility and speed, his ability to escape from the most secure (or so I thought) areas, his protectiveness of our house and family – all qualities of Rat Terriers! The only thing that differed was the lifespan. Most articles I read said that this breed can live up to about 12 – 18 years, but Flash lived to an amazing 22 years of age.

Being a Rat Terrier, one of Flash's life goals was to catch a squirrel. Unfortunately they were always just too quick for him, but that never deterred him from trying. It was as though he could sense when they were nearby, and just started charging in their direction, even if that direction was up a tree.

On the topic of small, furry creatures, our neighbour's daughter had two gorgeous Angora rabbits, which she kept in a cage outside their house (I'm sure you can already tell how this is going to end – badly).

During one of his excursions, Flash must have discovered the rabbits in their cage. And one very awkward morning, there was a knock on the door, and I opened it to find a very angry neighbour and his sobbing daughter. The neighbour told me that both rabbits had been killed by an animal which they were certain was Flash.

Apparently Flash had managed to get into the cage, and killed the younger rabbit. The older rabbit then died of a heart attack after witnessing the event. I didn't know what to say to them, but later that day I went to the pet shop and bought them another Angora rabbit.

Years later, a friend of mine met that neighbour and he told her this story. He also told her that he actually wasn't too upset about the loss of the two rabbits, as he was never that fond of them anyway. But what really upset him was when I had bought them a replacement rabbit, and Flash had apparently killed it as well. But he never told me about that incident.

This is not the end of Flash's rabbit encounters. Jump forward to my daughter's tenth birthday, when we hired a magician to perform at her party.

Everything was running smoothly, but I noticed that Flash kept barking and trying to get into the room where the magician's props were being stored. Eventually I had to lock him in another room, as he was scratching on the door to get in.

Later I discovered that the magician had a live rabbit, which he used for one of his tricks. As he pulled it out of his hat, I imagined how that rabbit could have looked if Flash had gotten hold of it, and the horrific turn the party would have taken. Thank goodness I'd kept him away.

After the Angora rabbit debacle, we realised that Flash didn't just venture out during the day, but at night as well. And I could never figure out how he kept doing it – I checked the perimeter fence regularly, and resealed all the possible escape routes I could find, but somehow he just kept getting out.

There was one night in particular, when Barbara was playing bridge at the local bridge club, and I was out with a friend.

At about 9:30 pm I received a frantic call from Barbara, saying that Flash was being held at the Pinner police station, and I needed to meet her there as soon as possible.

I raced to the police station, and walked in to find a smartly-dressed woman shouting at Barbara about Flash. While this was going on, I caught a glimpse of Flash in the yard, chained to a post like a criminal.

Apparently he had been on one of his evening walks, and while passing this lady's house, he'd caught the scent of her dog, who was on heat.

He snuck into the house through the cat flap, found the dog in question, and had gotten intimate with her, when the owner walked in on them.

The owner, still shouting, explained that her dog was of very high pedigree, or at least had been, before Flash got involved.

Lucky for us, the police saw the funny side of the situation. But they were still sympathetic towards the lady, and reprimanded me for not keeping Flash locked up. I kept a look out over the next couple of months for some half pedigree half mongrel puppies, but didn't see any wandering around…

Flash was very protective of our family, and did his best to guard the house. So he wasn't very happy when we just allowed strangers inside, despite his barking and protesting. He worked so hard to keep us safe, and here we were opening the door and letting in potentially dangerous individuals.

For instance, the carpenter that we hired to fix the bar in our lounge. Flash took an immediate dislike to him. He would watch, or rather stalk, him from the shadows, and when he was too busy measuring or cutting to notice his surroundings, Flash would pounce, attacking out of nowhere.

The carpenter did not appreciate this the first time it happened, never mind the third or fourth, and eventually quit the job. Flash seemed very proud that he'd managed to save us from this terrible intruder.

It wasn't just the carpenter, of course. Flash had a number of people on his hit list. He intensely disliked the accountant who lived three houses away from us, and would often watch and wait till he got out of his car, before making a dash for him. It was not uncommon for me to have to replace a torn pair of trousers.

Chapter 4
Friends and family

As Flash got older, Barbara decided that it would be a good idea to get another dog to keep him company. However, this time, rather than finding another rescue (with or without a limp), she had her heart set on a Bull Terrier, a breed that she had always loved. I told her I didn't think this was a good idea, but she insisted, and found a breeder with pups for sale.

So off we went to fetch our new dog.

We explained to the breeder that we already had another dog, and she assured us that a female puppy would be a good companion for Flash. She then asked if we wanted to meet the puppy's father, which I thought could be useful, as it might give an indication as to how big she would get. We went out into the back garden, and the breeder said she would fetch the father, but that I was not to move. So I stayed put, feeling a bit puzzled, until I saw an absolute titan of a dog come hurtling towards me, coming to an abrupt halt at my side. There was no need for the breeder's instructions – at this point I was honestly too scared to move. I breathed a huge sigh of relief when she took him back and I could return inside.

We took the puppy, Veronica, which was thankfully much smaller and less scary than her father, and brought her home to meet Flash. But when we tried to introduce them, Flash didn't seem overly interested in his new friend. The puppy, on the other hand, was full of energy, jumping around him, eager to play.

Flash began to spend more and more time upstairs. Whenever he ventured downstairs, Veronica would be waiting. She just wanted to play (as puppies do), but Flash was not interested in playing with her, and would eventually get angry and retaliate. These retaliations were clearly more warnings than actual attacks, as Flash could definitely have done more damage to this small puppy if he'd wanted to, but he never hurt her – just tried to make it very clear that he did not want to play.

But Veronica did not seem to pick up on this message, and over time these interactions escalated. It soon got to the stage where the two dogs could not be in the same room together. Flash had become very territorial and would attack Veronica if she got too close to him. Veronica, however, still thought that this was part of the game, and was happy to be playing with her friend. Being a Bull Terrier, she was never really in danger of getting hurt, but it was still a very difficult situation.

One night, just before we left for a wedding, the two dogs were having a full-on fight, and I was forced to step in and physically separate them. Thankfully, a quick scan of my black tie attire showed no scratch or tear marks, so I locked Flash in the upstairs room, and off we went to the wedding.

After a painfully long reception, we finally made it to the first course, after which we were all invited to join the bride and groom on the dance floor. It was a warm evening, so I took off my jacket, and noticed Barbara staring at me in horror. I looked down to find that my shirt was covered in blood. It would seem that when separating the dogs earlier, I hadn't quite made it out unscathed.

I made a speedy exit to the bathroom, trying to come up with a solution. Luckily, one of the guests who was staying in the hotel saw how I looked, and offered to lend me a shirt. I explained that I had gotten caught up in a dog fight, but I'm still not quite sure if he believed me.

After that awful night I realised that Flash and Veronica just weren't working out – things were only getting more and more tense and potentially violent. So the following evening, while Barbara was out playing bridge, I phoned the breeder and explained the situation. I told her that the two dogs were just not compatible, and that the growling and fighting was escalating, and I asked if it would be possible to bring Veronica back. She was very understanding, and said it would be alright, so off I went with Veronica, back to her original home. She seemed excited to be around dogs that were actually happy to interact with her – her father and a few of her siblings – so that was a relief. And I was also relieved that peace and quiet would finally return to our home, even though trying to get a friend for Flash turned out to be a very expensive mistake.

The next morning I was met by some teary faces, as my children cried about Veronica's departure, but they did agree that it was for the best – both for Flash, and our collective sanity and wellbeing. Flash, on the other hand, spent some time sniffing and

sneaking around to make sure that Veronica really was no longer there, and very happily reclaimed all the areas of the house that he had been avoiding.

But just because our attempt at finding Flash a friend was unsuccessful, doesn't mean that he didn't have any friends in the neighbourhood. I remember that for a while Flash would disappear, sometimes for two days at a time, with us having no idea where he'd gone. This was also in his later years, so we were pretty worried, in case something had happened or he'd been injured.

So I decided to follow him the next time he snuck out. As you probably imagine, this proved to be much more difficult than I'd expected. Even though he was older he was still very quick and agile, and tended to choose routes which were far better suited to dogs than humans. But eventually, after chasing him down some alleyways and along narrow footpaths, I finally discovered where he'd been sneaking off to – another house in our neighbourhood, not too far from our own.

I went up to the house and knocked on the door, and was greeted by two loud barks. And when the owner opened the door, I found two dogs staring at me, wagging their tails – Flash and his new friend.

It turns out Flash and this other dog had met somewhere in the neighbourhood, and the two of them had become fast friends. And when the owner found them both playing around his house, he decided to let Flash stay the night, as he didn't know where he came from or who he belonged to. I apologised for Flash's bad behaviour, but was relieved to know that he was safe, and that he had managed to make a friend. This other dog was also a Jack Russel cross, and the two of them really did seem to get on very well, so the other owner and I exchanged numbers and agreed to arrange some playdates. It would certainly be better for our anxiety and peace of mind, knowing they weren't sneaking off to see each other.

As great as it was for Flash to have a dog friend, I sometimes wonder if Flash even knew he was a dog. As I mentioned earlier, he was so much a part of our family, that he was practically one of the children. And he definitely acted like it. He was also very protective of our three children, Justine, Carla, and Richard, and would do just about anything to keep them safe.

However, if he had a favourite sibling, it would probably be my son Richard. Right from when Richard was born, it was clear that there was a bond between the two of them, that lasted up until the day Flash died. Flash also decided that Richard's room was the most comfortable, and commandeered his couch as his bed to sleep on every night. We thought this was extremely cute, but poor Richard said it led to many sleepless nights, as Flash was a very loud snorer.

Flash also loved to get involved in all the children's activities – he always wanted to be part of the fun – and he can be seen in many group photos with our children and their friends.

My daughter Carla would also spend a lot of time with Flash, using him as her personal therapist. She would sit with him for hours, telling him about all her thoughts and troubles. He was either very attentive, or just liked the attention, but either way it seemed to help.

Chapter 5
Older, but not wiser

Flash, although fearless, was a bit like a naughty child – needlessly defiant and refusing to listen. Usually negative qualities, but this disobedience actually helped a friend of mine to start his business, in a somewhat roundabout way.

It was a beautiful Sunday morning and the sun was shining, so we decided to make the most of it and go for a walk down the High Street. But things took a rather bleak turn when we made the mistake of letting Flash off the lead. He instantly went bounding across the road to the other side of the street. The more I yelled for him to stop, the more he thought it was a game and kept running.

Then he disappeared out of sight, and the next thing we heard was the screeching of brakes, followed by a thud.

We raced towards the sound, and found Flash, lying on the side of the road, with a large gash in his side. The owner of the car was in a state, saying that she was so sorry, but she just couldn't stop in time.

We bundled Flash up as fast as we could, and found an emergency vet in Hendon. The vet said that he would stitch him up and do what he could, but warned us that due to Flash's age, this was a risky procedure, and there was a chance that he wouldn't last the night.

That was one of the longest nights of my life. I couldn't sleep at all, from the worry and fear. I just kept waiting for a devastating phone call, with terrible news. Preparing myself for the worst. The whole family was upset and on edge, waiting.

But the phone call never came, and the next day when we returned to the vet, we were beyond surprised to find that Flash was not just alive, but back on his feet! The vet said it was a miracle that he survived, and that he was, amazingly, already well enough to go home. He gave us some medicine for the next few days, and put Flash in a lampshade collar to prevent him from biting his stitches, and we left, overjoyed that Flash managed to pull through and was on the road to recovery.

And it seems this road to recovery was more of an alley, or very short lane to recovery, as within about a week he was already back to his usual self. He even managed to escape while wearing the lampshade collar (which the children had named the "collar of shame"). We panicked when we realised he was gone, as the collar gave him a very restricted view, and the thought of him being knocked over again was just too much to bear! After hours of searching we eventually found him, wandering along Pinner High Street. I still have no idea how he managed to escape, lampshade collar and all.

I did say that something good came out of this story, and that was the start of MediVet. Asher, a friend of mine who had recently immigrated to the UK, was a vet, and he was currently in search of a practice. I mentioned to him that the vet who had treated Flash was rather old, and possibly close to retirement, and suggested that he contact him.

He ended up buying the practice and starting the MediVet group. I attribute this almost entirely to Flash's accident, due to his blatant disobedience.

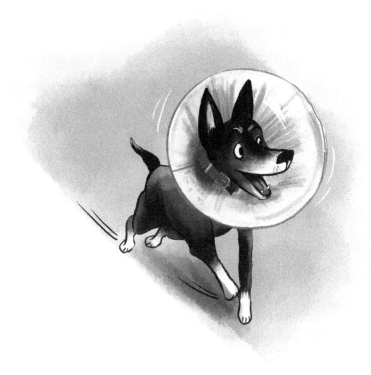

I told you that when I first laid eyes on Flash I didn't think he was particularly handsome. Well his looks took a turn for the worse one winter, when friends from Canada came to stay with us over Christmas. I distinctly remember it being very cold and windy.

We had just arrived home, when one of our guests realised he'd dropped a glove outside, so went out to retrieve it. As he stepped back inside a gust of wind caused the door to slam shut behind him with such force, that it shattered the glass frame above it. This meant shards of glass flying in all directions, and Flash was unfortunately in the firing line of one of these. The piece of glass whizzed past and sliced off the tip of his ear. Luckily it wasn't serious, but it certainly added character to his appearance.

As Flash got older, he became more and more aggressive.

On one occasion, he attacked an old woman on her bicycle outside our house, causing her to fall off and hurt her leg.

Then there was the time when I answered the door to find a policeman standing there. Angrily, he showed me his ripped trousers and the puncture marks on his ankle. Flash was now standing next to me, of course, wagging his tail and looking as innocent as possible.

The policeman told me he was going to report the incident, as Flash was now a dangerous dog. I phoned my friend Asher, the vet, to ask for some advice. He recommended that Flash be castrated, as this should calm him down and make him less aggressive.

So he had the operation, and there was a noticeable decrease in his aggression.

But three weeks later I still received a summons to appear in Harrow court, on the charges of harbouring a dangerous dog.

Not knowing what to do, I contacted a friend who was a barrister, and explained the situation to him. He said that it would be ridiculous if he were to appear in court defending a dog, so he told me that I would need to do it myself. His advice was to put on a suit and look respectable, and defend Flash as best I could.

I still remember that day clearly.

I put on my best suit, and carried a briefcase which didn't have much in it, but I felt it made me look more credible.

When I arrived at the court, I had some trouble parking, but eventually found a meter, and rushed into the building. There were a number of people waiting, so I approached the court warden to ask when my case would be heard. She explained that there was a queue, and that she would call me when it was my turn. I was feeling rather agitated, as I still had patients to see, and needed to get back to the surgery, but there wasn't much I could do about the situation, so I took a seat and tried to wait as patiently as I could.

After about half an hour of waiting, someone came up to me and said that they had opened another court down the corridor, and that I should go there.

I picked up my briefcase and ran to the other courtroom. As I stepped inside I saw three magistrates looking at me.

A few moments passed and no one spoke, so I thought I would get things started. I proceeded to explain that since the castration he is much more docile and no longer bites people like he used to. He mostly just stays at home now.

I stopped to catch my breath, and noticed that the magistrates were looking at me in utter bewilderment. Then one of them finally spoke, and asked me what I was talking about. It was then that I noticed a man standing next to me. Apparently he had been arrested for drunk driving, and they thought that I was the lawyer representing him. This man looked very confused, which I suppose is understandable, considering I had just told the magistrates that he had been castrated. They seemed to find the situation quite amusing though, and asked me to return when they were done dealing with the drunk driving case.

Luckily, I think that this blunder worked in my favour, as they let Flash off with a suspended sentence.

You will remember that when we adopted Flash, he allegedly had a limp, caused by being thrown from a car. The limp might have been alleged, but the being thrown from a car was unfortunately true, and probably the reason that he hated driving in the car.

One December we went on holiday to Cape Town, to visit family and friends. I needed to get back earlier for work, so I left Barbara and the children to enjoy the Cape Town summer, while I returned to freezing cold and snowy London. It was just me and Flash for two days until they arrived back.

I had to go to the surgery in Ealing that morning but knew I couldn't leave Flash in the house by himself, so I decided to take him with me to the surgery. I knew he disliked the car, but the alternative was leaving him alone in the freezing cold house.

We started out, and I saw that there was ice on the road, making an already difficult journey more dangerous. But once we were on the A4 highway, the roads were safer, and I felt more secure. I could see, however, that Flash was agitated, so instinctively I opened the window so that he could get some air. By now you can probably tell where this is going. I don't need to explain that it was a huge mistake.

Of course, Flash saw this as an opportunity to escape, and somehow managed to jump out of the window, onto the busy highway. I immediately tried to pull over, at the same time trying not to cause an accident or pile up, which is not an easy task, and not something I'd want to do again. But thankfully the drivers behind me saw what had happened, and helped to stop the oncoming cars.

And luckily, due to the snowfall, Flash had difficulty running, so I was able to reach him before he got run over.

Another disaster narrowly avoided, caused, as usual, by Flash the menace.

When we went on holiday, my decorator, Simon, would dog sit for us. He absolutely loved Flash, and was happy to do a combination of decorating and dog sitting when we were away. In fact, we would try to plan our holidays for when we needed some decorating done, to be as efficient as possible.

He especially loved taking Flash for walks, but told me about one frightening occasion where both he and Flash nearly drowned.

Near the house there was a lake that used to freeze over in winter. On this specific occasion, while out walking, he decided to let Flash off the lead. I'm sure alarm bells are already going off in your head.

Flash started running towards some birds sitting on the frozen lake, and the thin ice gave way, plunging Flash into the freezing water. Simon had no choice but to jump in to rescue him. Luckily the lake was shallow enough that he was able to stand and wade through the water, and save Flash. But he told me that he ended up with a terrible cold that took two weeks to get over.

Chapter 6
The final chapter

Flash was now 22 years old, or 154 in dog years, which I'm sure you'll agree is pretty remarkable.

But he was also showing his age, finding it difficult to climb up stairs, or onto the bed. It had got to the point where we even had to carry him outside to relieve himself.

It was a cold winter morning, and Flash began howling. We realised he must be in a lot of pain.

We took him to our local MediVet branch, where we had been taking him for many years now. The staff were always happy to see Flash – he had become something of a local hero at the clinic, with the largest file by far. They were always amazed at how he was still going strong after all these years. But this time was different. We knew that Flash was not well. The vet told us that all his organs were shutting down and that he was dying. He said that the best thing to do at this point would be to put him out of his misery.

We knew this moment would come someday, but that didn't make it any easier to hear, or make us any more prepared to deal with it. But we understood that he was suffering, and that this was the best thing that we could do for him. I stayed with Flash throughout the procedure, so that he wasn't alone. I watched the vet administer the injection, and a minute later I saw his eyes close. He was gone. But I knew he was at peace.

I removed his red collar, which I still have to this day. I then left the room, and as I walked into the waiting area I was greeted by my family all in tears.

We all deal with grief in different ways. That day I drank half a bottle of scotch, and played the most awful golf with my son.

The vet asked if we would like to bury Flash or have him cremated. We decided to have him cremated, and received his ashes in a small, decorative box, with a plaque bearing his name. I kept the box in my study on the top shelf – a prime location.

Chapter 7

Beyond the final chapter

About a week after Flash had died, strange things began to happen.

One night, while lying in bed, I heard a dog barking outside. The bark was familiar, and without really thinking I assumed it was Flash, so went downstairs to open the door for him. I then remembered that Flash had died a week earlier.

But I kept hearing barking at random times. I decided it must be my imagination playing tricks on me, and tried to put it out of my mind.

Then one day Barbara was playing bridge in our kitchen with some friends, when one of them asked her if she had a dog. Surprised, she asked why. The friend said she felt something brush past her leg, and thought it was a dog. Barbara explained that she used to have a dog, but that it had died recently, so the lady must have imagined it.

Then there was a truly strange occurrence. I had got into the habit of getting my hair cut at home, by a great hairdresser who was happy to come to the house. But he told me that he was moving to Leeds, so I was looking for someone new. Barbara had got a recommendation from her manicurist, for a good hairdresser who does home visits, and trusting this recommendation, I decided to set up an appointment.

I remember that evening so well. Diane the hairdresser arrived, and we chatted for a while, making small talk, and discussing my hairstyle. She seemed very friendly.

After washing my hair, I sat down so that she could begin combing and cutting it. But after a few minutes she suddenly put the scissors down. She looked pale and frightened, and without an explanation, quickly packed up her equipment and literally ran out of the house.

Barbara heard the door slam, and was impressed with the speed of the haircut, until I told her what had happened. I assured her that I hadn't been rude or done anything to offend Diane, and that I had no idea why she acted the way she did.

The next day Barbara was seeing her manicurist, and she mentioned Diane's strange behaviour. The manicurist told her that Diane was a very spiritual person, and that she probably felt a supernatural or threatening force telling her that she wasn't welcome.

We later found out that she had felt the presence of a creature looking down at her while she was cutting my hair. She had been cutting my hair in my study, where the box with Flash's remains was sitting on the top shelf, looking down on us. Part of me thought that perhaps Flash was trying to protect me, from someone attacking me with scissors. But who knows...

After all of these incidents, Barbara decided to call a family meeting. And on a Sunday morning, we scattered his ashes in the garden, where he loved to play.

There were no more incidents after that.
Flash was finally free and at peace.

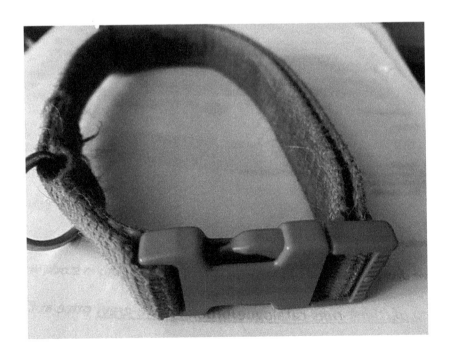

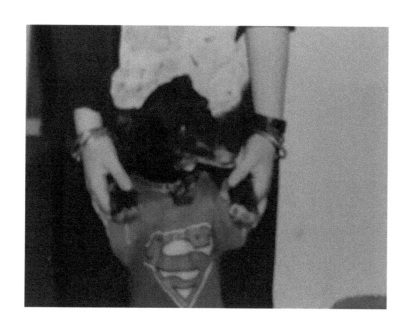

The End